Sacred
Intimacy

Sacred Intimacy

by

C. Suzanne Deakins

One Spirit Press
Portland, Oregon

Copyrighted 2010 by C.Suzanne Deakins

All rights reserved.
Printed in the USA

ISBN 978-1-893075-49-8
LCCN: 2007903103

Cover Art and Design by Ethan Firpo
Book Design Spirit Press

This book may not be reproduced by electronic or any other means which exist now or may yet be developed, without permission of Spirit Press, except in the case of brief quotations embodied in critical articles and reviews.

One Spirit Press
onespiritpress.com
Portland, Oregon

Table of Contents

Introduction..............vi

Beginnings.............3

Sacred Spaces.............13

Nakedness.............21

Sensuality.............29

Touch.............35

Forgiveness.............45

Self.............51

Covenants.............57

God.............61

Power.............69

Surrender.............77

Passion.............85

Absolute Love.............91

Joy.............97

Relationships.............103

Silk and Sandlewood............119

Colophon.............120

Introduction

If there ever was an idea that never grows old, is worth a fortune, and is sought by most people it would be love. The world is filled with people wanting to be loved. We torture our minds, souls, and bodies seeking love and acceptance by our partners. We teach our children about math, science, and history but we never teach them about the ideas they need for survival and happiness, intimacy and love.

Intimate...Indicative of ones deepest nature, essential, innermost to be very close as a friend or confidant

Looking into the eyes of my children and grandchildren, there is a kind of peace and love to be found there. My real first experience of love was looking into the face of my firstborn child. At that moment the face of God was revealed to me. An epiphany of eternity occurred when I realized that all life was conceived in love and continued in love. There is an intimacy about bearing a child, an attachment, and instinct that satisfies us. Perhaps Freud was right we search our entire lives for intimacy, connection, and existential existence we first felt with our mothers. Intimacy is so important to our health and well being that we die from the lack of it.

This is a book about intimacy and the part it plays in our longing for love, our sexuality, and desire for spiritual love and a sacred space. It is about a desire that we often mistake for physical love. It is our desire for survival that pushes us to seek intimacy. The desire to be known by our lovers and loved in a spiritual space pushes us toward intimacy. This writing is about what I have learned and know to be so about the nature of reality, of intimacy and love.

Hopefully, as you read, you will keep a journal... write down your thoughts... perhaps keep a love journal. By keeping track of your thoughts on intimacy and love ... moments you feel love you will begin to reveal to yourself your inner most thoughts and hopes. In our darkest times we often forget that we have known love and intimacy, maybe not the kind of love we desire, but others have loved us and we have loved. Being able to recognize love is the first step in loving and being loved.

Love is an active verb. It gives motion and meaning to our lives, communication, and spiritual desires. Love does not come without movement a reaching out and receiving. For Intimacy to be present in our lives we must seek it, accept it, and give it. It is a flow of energy from in-to-out. To experience true intimacy we must stand emotionally naked before our lovers unafraid of what will be. We must allow our very nature to dilate into the universal consciousness proclaiming our being and connection to all life.

Intimacy and love are not the same idea. Sex and love are not the same idea and sex and intimacy are not the same. They are all components of consciousness. We can only write and communicate through our consciousness. As you read this book you are reading my consciousness of intimacy. In writing this book much was revealed to me about intimacy, love, and sacred spaces where intimacy occurs.

All acts of intimacy acts of spirituality, of creative energy and sexuality. Sex does not have to culminate in a physical act of coupling but is definitely present in all that we do. Some of my ideas and discoveries may sound strange and unreal to you. Hopefully as you read you will set aside the beliefs you hold as sacred cows get past what you believe, to have a revelation about love and being loved in the most intimate ways. It is my experience that only through revelation do we change our consciousness and our worldview. As we change our consciousness and our perception our world experiences changes.

Experience tells us touch is essential if a child or animal is too survive it most be touched. It must be touched with love if it is to express love in a meaningful and nonviolent way as an adult. We think of love as coming from the heart. But love also comes from the head. To think with the heart and feel with the mind is the way of the masters, the priestess... the mother/father of all.

Finally, it seems that as a species we seek to know and be known in an intimate way that reveals the core of our being, our creator source. Perhaps all acts of love, sex, and intimacy are simply acts of self-remembering the Truth of us, the God... the reality of being absolute love.

Intimacy of all kinds can only happen in a sacred space. Sacred spaces are created between individuals who reach out beyond the earth bound chrysalis to a greater idea. We reach for a state of consciousness that says we emanate from the same idea, the core of all life, timeless, space-less and eternal Truth. Intimacy can only occur in a sacred space, a space created out of our desire to know and be known spiritually in our true state of being.

Gratitude

I hold a deep gratitude to my friends, clients, and family. They revealed many thoughts on intimacy and sacredness. Crossing the hot sands of the desert, jumping the great chasm of insanity and finally filling our existential voids we found peace and direction in our conversations. It is really impossible to explain the process and the sense of joy and gratitude that came with those who were willing to expose their inner most being.

There are too many people to thank... on this page. Please know that each conversation, each revelation has been cherished.

C. Suzanne Denkins

August 29, 2010
West Linn, Oregon

Dedicated

To my mother and father, brother and his family and my children. To all of those who have shared my journey. To David Fishman at ACIMGather for his graciousness and enthusiasm about the topic. To Billye Talmadge who taught me to feel with my mind freeing me to explore my intimacy.

To be intimate with an individual, an idea or Truth/God we must create a sacred space. All intimacy is sacred.

Sacred Intimacy

Beginnings

Many people seek intimacy through sexual expression. It appears that sexuality is one of the easiest and best ways of being intimate for a split second, but by no means the only path to true intimacy. If intimacy occurs before sexual encounter the participants can then reach a peak of intimacy that is much greater than just an orgasm. When intimacy occurs before a sexual encounter a sacred space may be created for the individuals. This sacred space is a necessary place for men and women to feel whole and complete and unafraid. It is in this sacred space that we remember our true identity, Truth. For a sexual encounter to be more than just a hedonistic act of sexual release there must be a sacred space. This space must be created by each of those participating.

In orgasm we are open and not separate for one intense moment. This leads up to a moment that breaks down the walls that exist in our psychic centers and our emotional life. It removes fear, assault of self, and the need to devour. In trying to be intimate many people emotionally devour partners and lovers. This devouring is the drive to be intimate to enter into the sacred space of knowing the God self of the individual. Because we are not taught intimacy, love, and creation of sacredness, we often misdirect our energy and attention. Intimacy is so vital to our health –physical and emotional– that we seek it out. This seeking is at an unconscious level.

We seek emotional connections similar to the way we seek food that contains the essential vitamins and minerals needed for our health. Intimacy is primal need in our system. It is perhaps more primal and phylogentic than sex itself. Perhaps Maslow missed the importance of intimacy in his hierarchy of needs. The need for intimacy should follow the needs for air, water, food and safety. Intimacy is a survival need in our unconscious mind. We often seek to satisfy this need through sexual coupling. If not through sex how do we express intimacy in our daily lives? I hope by the time you have finished this book you will have an answer to the expression of intimacy.

True intimacy and its sacredness is created in a state of absolute Truth/Love. We all have loved and do love many people. Love is absolute, no matter what the emotional attachment it is eter-

nal and the very basis of all creation. Our focus of love may change but love is eternal. Once we recognize we love an individual that love is not taken from us, but remains a part of our psychic and consciousness throughout eternity.

All love is sacred and somewhat emotional. Love is often emotional because the very use of the word love sets off a cascade of endorphins in our body and mind. So what do we mean when we say, I love you? The word love carries as many meanings as those who use the word. This means we can't give it a particular meaning, but we can give some general denotations of what we mean when we use it. To understand what we mean when we use the word love we need to comprehend what causes us to say I love you.

Most of our emotional behavior is based on need. That is we respond emotionally to situations and people because of our needs or what our mind feels is needed for survival. Some of these needs are archetypical in nature. That is they are symbols deep seeded in our unconscious mind and universal in their meanings.

The concept of love or saying I love you is in every culture in the world. Of course it takes on different meanings and uses according to the social ideation of the individual. Just as the concept of houses or shelter is common throughout our world so is the concept of love. This would mean that a concept of love is as important for survival as shelter. Survival needs attend the ongoing physical life of an individual and their well being.

Simple experiments done in the late 1960's at the University of Southern California demonstrated the importance of emotional attachment to the growth of plants. The experiments showed that a simple use of the word love and gently touching the rows of corn in an existential way was important to the growth. Rows of corn that were talked to in terms of love and stroked in a loving way grew larger than the corn left alone under identical physical conditions. Cursing at and withholding emotional connection from rows of corn caused them to produce ears of corn that were small and deformed. This seems to mean that love or what it means to us at an unconscious level is important at all levels of existence.

The importance of understanding this need for intimacy and love has been even more apparent in recent intentional experiments preformed throughout the world. These have shown that even standing near a plant with certain intentions can effect the growth and how plants use the light and nutrition. From plants, to water and not least to animals and people, love and intimacy are important parts of survival.

New born babies at risk are held in neonatal units in hospitals, stroked and spoken too. The caretaker, parent or surrogate, creates and intimate bond with the new born infant that assures it that survival is worth the fight. This beginning intimate bond teaches the new being the emotional and ontological connections between themselves and the world. It is a natural part of the existential extension that helps the infants consciousness cross the seeming voids created by the expulsion from the womb.

The stronger the intimate bond between infant and caretaker the more self-reliant and confident the child will grow. Its actions will be of accepting and curiosity about the world rather than retreat and defensiveness. A child who is intimately connected to another being brings a sense of peace to their life, is capable of acts of love and gentleness. The child who lacks this kind of intimate bond suffers with bouts of paranoia and fear of what awaits them. The child who lacks this sacred beginning intimacy is unable to connect to others and life in a purposeful way.

At the moment of birth we begin building a sacred intimacy with our mother and later with those who would care for us and love us. Nothing teaches a parent more about love than those first few moments after birth seeing the life they have nurtured and brought into manifestation. What is love? An emotional attachment seems

an inadequate definition for what appears to be a part of our human survival. Saying I love you must mean I need you in some manner for my continuing survival. I need not to feel separate... I want to be intimate in some manner with you. We know that for most people separation and the lack of intimacy for long periods of time causes havoc in life... it leads to a break down in our immune system and we loose our connection to our body and find it hard to stay present and alert.

Saying I love you produces a connection of emotional intimacy and an acknowledgment of existence on a common emotional plane. It is as needed as fruit and vegetables in our diet to keep us healthy. Saying I love you is saying I recognize your existence; I am willing to communicate with you... I am willing to allow you to know me. When I tell my children I love you, I am saying I know you, feel connected to you and I know you feel the connection and can know me.

Because of the importance of these simple words carries impacts we can't begin to describe. Saying I love you cures, heals, and produces joy. It cannot be said too much for the very word love creates a vibration in our being that neutralizes fear, hate, and insanity.

Each time we say I love you we create a stronger intimate bond with those who are close to us. The drive to love and be loved, to be intimate, to be known emotionally and spiritually is very strong in all of us. The need cannot be denied. Perhaps insanity and mental illness are nothing more than the lack of intimate connections. And understanding that need may be the magic pill we all look for.

Fear is a closing off, seeing life outside of your self, while love and intimacy are the opposite of fear. Like light and dark are of the same fabric so are love and fear. When another says I love you they say I am here, I hear you, I am emotionally naked and not hiding from our connection. Fear is often love withheld, intimacy not experienced. If love has been tainted with pain and hurt we will fear it as much as we desire it. In ontological therapy we look for those moments in our life where the paradox exists. This paradox allows us to experience something outside of previous understanding. We can step outside of normal consciousness into the forest of unfulfilled categories.

The paradox of wanting love and intimacy and fearing it is the point where we can self remember our true being... the paradox in itself puts our ego to sleep long enough for the higher consciousness, the Truth, the God within, to come forth producing an epiphany or metanioa

(change of mind) that literally shifts the whole consciousness. In turn this shift brings about a new perception of love and intimacy in our life. Our experiences then will reflect this shift in consciousness.

The fear of being naked (emotionally and psychically) in the presence of our lovers (Lovers being all of those who love us and we love and isn't meant sexually.), stems from our feelings of guilt of not being good enough for the connection. We fear that our being is soiled in some manner, that our thoughts of self loathing and guilt will be revealed to the other. We misunderstand the concept of perfection thinking that our human idea of perfection is that of Truth/God. Humanity sees perfection as the rose without the thorn. Creation says I am whole and complete and rose is perfect thorn and all. The perfection of being has nothing to do with physical appearance, emotional maturity or spiritual achievement. Perfection deals with the wholeness, completeness. Truth/God is whole and perfect. Is all there is and nothing else is needed. It is perfection. This is important because when we reach for perfection we get caught in our beliefs and fears of not being worthy.

We are the effect of the creator source. As a book is written in the mind from the creativity of the author and bread is baked from the creative aspect of a baker...the essence of the creator is in

the progeny be it a book, bread, or humanity. In this we are of the nature of the creator source, whole, complete, and perfect.

Being told we are loved and saying I love you can lower the level of fear and hormones that destroy our bodies and minds. Saying I love you says simply, I feel connected to you... I want you to love me and feel connected to me. Intimacy and love are basic survival needs. Both must be present for a sacred connection to occur between individuals.

To be intimate with an individual, an idea or Truth/God we must create a sacred space. All intimacy is sacred.

Intimacy occurs only in a sacred space. We aren't intimate with our bodies, but with our minds especially when we surrender to the true self.

Sacred Spaces

Relationships, lovers, marriages, and families all need sacred space. A sacred space is by definition a place dedicated and devoted entirely to the deity or the work of the deity. What does this mean? It means that to be intimate, to know ourselves as whole and perfect in the nature of reality, we must acknowledge that place we call divine and or deity. It does not matter if you call this place, God, Buddha, Divine Mind, Supra Consciousness, Truth or any other word. If you can't acknowledge that which is so about yourself and the other you can't create a sacred space.

That which is so about any individual is the timeless and spaceless expression of being. When you understand that even to say I don't exist is to say I AM or I am being or existing. This is the true nature of all humankind. In this recognition you are distinguishing that which is

divine in your nature and the nature of others. When acknowledging the higher self, the deity, the God self in others and ourselves we allow the spirit to be free to connect and create what we need for our awakening consciousness.

If you ask a child what is special about their parents they will use ideas such as they give me treats, they are warm or they give me milk. Children are specific and they relate to their life in a very sensory way. They are learning to negotiate there body and physical setting. Many adults answer similarly. They relate to the physical aspect of a partner or love object as if they were still children. We seem to grow in our knowledge of math, the world but in relationships we often remain stunted and unable to reach beyond our childhood beliefs.

That which attracts us to another being is rarely their physical being. Perhaps the physical being gets our attention but in the end if we are in a relationship of any sort based on physical aspects only, we are doomed in that the physical is temporal. We change as we age and life changes. Love and intimacy must be based on something that is changeless, enduring and always so. Love and intimacy must be based on that which has always been so, will always be so …eternally present NOW.

I

Sacred Intimacy

ntimacy in true relationships celebrates the spirit, the Truth expressed by the "other." A true intimacy celebrates the shifting sands of the physical world... embraces the unfolding of consciousness. Each moment is spent in a kind of awakening of joy and peace. This does not mean there aren't occasionally conflicts of ideas, and disagreements. But these moments aren't symptoms of a relationship gone off track, but rather the paradoxes that unfold as our consciousness unfolds into greater realms of understanding.

Intimacy occurs only in a sacred space. We aren't intimate with our bodies, but with our minds particularly when we surrender to the true self. This place of intimacy is created in a sacred space of our thoughts. That is within our thinking, within what scientist call the God Center of our mind we must be willing to accept that all life is from the Creator.

The Creator is consciousness. This Creator has been given many names through the ages. BUT in the end we must acknowledge that all life is from our consciousness. It is through our consciousness that we acknowledge and accept life. The Creator in Western terms is God the Father. The Creator of life appears in many forms throughout our world, in Paganism it is God the Mother. In Eastern philosophy it often appears as Kwan Yin (the androgynous being that appears as the bringer of life) and Buddha. These all represent aspects of our consciousness of the

very energy we define as life and presence of the other.

The acknowledgement that each and every atom and molecule is made in the image of God/the Creator is important in creating a sacred place for intimacy to occur. It does not matter how you define the higher being or higher consciousness or God. It does, however, matter that you acknowledge that beyond all illusion of person, place, time, and thing, life itself is the progeny of the Creator, of consciousness. How we view the world through our beliefs is how the world appears to us. Our beliefs dictate our experiences and life view.

Many of us were taught that the Creator (God) is good. We were also taught we are not God and therefore not good. This belief that we are not God or God consciousness prevents us from understanding the nature of reality and the God-self (Creator) present in all life.

The Western Bible says for the Gods created in their image, as the creators (Gods) our consciousness prescribes how the world is to be viewed. If we understand these statements as statements of consciousness then we can understand that consciousness replicates its beliefs in the world that is presented to our senses. We must acknowledge that we are the Creator/God through our beliefs and consciousness before we can accept the God self of any other person.

The God self creates the sacred spaces. Creating anything for instance a sacred space, a meal, painting or a piece of music has two main aspects. We must surrender our ego self to principles we seek to express and accept our creation. Sacred space and intimacy can only be the Creator creating in the state of mind of surrender and acceptance. We must know that all we view is our consciousness and that consciousness is the Creator and God, there for all life is an experience of God.

In this creating of sacred space the sanctified male/female aspect of all life is awakened. Our androgynous nature must act in that we must both want and accept our desires of intimacy and revered relationships. The androgynous self knows only absolute love, experiences only that which is whole, complete and prefect in its expression of all life. It is only from this state of being that a sacred space exists.

If we separate our self from deity we find ourselves outside of the garden of life. Intimacy is an act of higher being, God, Creator, Higher mind. You cannot be intimate in the (human) man state of being. In the Garden of Eden, Adam and Eve discovered the human (man state) of being. In this discovery they separated themselves from the God Self and then of course were expelled from the Garden, which represents the sacred space created by our God self. When at-

tention is placed on the human state of being our senses begin to believe what the sensations like a mirage in the desert. Once this happens we are expelled from the Garden or God Self sacred spaces.

Christ said you may only enter into the Kingdom of Heaven as a small child. Children instinctively live an existential life and in the Garden. Children see all life as sacred. There is not a decision on what is real and what is abstract. They just exist connected to all life.

What is meant by Christ statement is that until we know we are all life, that it is our beliefs that creates the worldview we experience we cannot enter back into the Garden or Heaven. It is this innocence that all life is the creation of the Creator the God consciousness that allows us to experience the whole and perfect existence of that which is so, that which is true about our self. If we don't acknowledge this we hide outside of the Garden of sacred space and intimacy.

The act of creating is the act of bringing the world into ordered existence. From the clouds of chaos comes divine order and purpose. Creation begins with the chaos of misunderstanding, illusion, and error. When we create we experience divine principle, axiomatic truths, and the essence of all life. In creation we find purpose and meaning beyond our beliefs and confusion. Creating a sacred space means you must clarify

your consciousness of the oasis of miss-belief. You must stand on the cliff of sanity having enough faith and trust in your innate sense of deity to take that step. You must be willing to give up old beliefs, all concepts of self for the ever living principle of the androgynous creator within. The Truth of us is neither male or female. The Truth of us is whole, complete, and perfect. We are the children of the creator source, God/Truth. We are spiritual beings, living in a spiritual universe governed by spiritual law.

There isn't someone sitting on a cloud directing our life or an astrology chart that dictates our fate. It is our consciousness that directs our life. This consciousness brings forth our purpose of being and commitment to sacredness. No one can take our consciousness away. It has always been and always will be. It is not sacredness or loving relationships that hide from us, but we in our confusion and fear that hide from the God/Truth.

Relationships with God/Truth are sacred, and the intimacy of knowing and experiencing only happens when we surrender our ego to that which is so in the nature of reality.

To become intimate with our God/Truth we must be naked and vulnerable, drop our worldly beliefs and roles to know we are pure consciousness aware of itself as consciousness.

Nakedness

The dichotomy of intimacy is that to be intimate we must pass through what we fear most. In many cases this is the fear of being known, and yet the only way to be intimate is to reveal our inner most self to those we love. When I was young and attending spiritual classes, I often stood in wonder at the teachers who could reach me. I finally saw that those who reached me, triggering me into an epiphany, were those who could stand unafraid of their knowledge and revelations before the students. Those teachers who expressed their vulnerable existence at any level reached their students. This for me was one of my first experiences with true intimacy.

An ontological teacher gives not of their knowledge but rather of spirit. They teach through their surrender to the Holy Spirit. To teach they must embrace their sanctified androgynous self. They must be vulnerable to both Truth and their

students. Anyone who does less than this is simply an instructor giving information.

Teaching is a kind of leadership it leads those who come to the doorway of their own mind. It does not dictate the language that must be used. It does not set ridged temporal laws. True teaching is based on axiomatic laws, which is spiritual law changeless and absolute love expressing through creation. A true teaching may bring fear to the surface of the student, but it does not use fear as a teacher. Absolute love as spiritual law does not tolerate madness and insanity for it seeks cohesion and fusion in all life. Like light, absolute love vanquishes the darkness of fear.

Fear and panic do terrible things to our bodies and emotional lives. Our cells close down and refuse to accept the food needed to sustain life; our mind closes and we can no longer think; pulse and heart rate go up; and our system is flooded with adrenal hormones that thwart our immune systems. Fear is a killer of consciousness. Once we are experiencing fear, our consciousness returns to a primal state of fight and flight. We revert to a primal state often associated with animal survival.

Finding a way out of fear can only happen when we become vulnerable to the state of consciousness that is expressing absolute love and your divine nature. The fear must pass through you

like you pass through a dark room. If you try to hold onto fear or control it, you simply increase the seeming power it holds. When we turn on the light in a dark room the corners and shadows are no longer monsters. This example applies to fear, once the light of consciousness is turned on the scary fear returns from the nothing from whence it came.

If we think in terms of mathematics we find a good example of how this works. 2+2=5 is a mistake or fear. It is wrong and when used causes an upset in our check books. When we shed the light of understanding on it, and know the axiomatic Truth (mathematical principles are axiomatic as they are so in all realms of our universe and are not temporal.) When we understand that 2+ 2=4 the error or fear of 2+2=5 returns to the nothingness it came from. It is nothing more than an illusion a misunderstanding and has no viability in the nature of reality.
To become intimate with our God/Truth we must be naked and vulnerable, drop our worldly beliefs and roles to know we are pure consciousness aware of itself as consciousness.

When we are unbridled consciousness aware of itself as consciousness, we are naked. Our ego cannot hide us. This means our roles and what we think we are in human terms are no longer applicable. We are without the roles and identities of the dramas we play out day-after-day in worldly perceptions.

Nakedness

When we feel attracted to another, we look beyond their roles and daily dramas to the truth of their existence. Just as with children, we don't buy the drama, the confusion, and misperception of life. We naturally seek the potential in others. We seek their nakedness. That is we seek their true identity that cannot be hidden under roles and worldly beliefs. When we fall in love we do not love the physical being, the roles of another but the beingness, the consciousness, and potential of the expression of intimacy. We love the naked appearance of life.

Getting naked is not easy. Seeing others naked (without their worldly concepts) can be embarrassing, but to be intimate, to feel for that one moment we are connected to all life, we are the expression of life we must become naked, that is vulnerable to the nature of reality. We must allow our self to just be.

To be naked emotionally means we must be open to changes in our emotions. We must drop the emotional safeguards, the roles we feel comfortable, in and allow ourselves to be. Easier said then done. By the time we reach high school we have built an ego of emotional roles.

As a child we reacted to things much differently than we do as adults. As children we build an emotional arsenal. This arsenal stays in place as an adult protecting us (so we think) from further pain and emotional injury. It is often said

when we are intimate and sexual with another it is as if we are two children playing. The ideas and beliefs we have about our emotional life are often those of children.

We are taught by our Western society that to be naked is sinful and bad. Even the smallest child is stuffed into a swimsuit to cover the body. We carry this shamefulness into our adult relationships. Relationships at every walk of life bear the consequences of this early shame drilled into us as children. Guilt and shame often hold hands with fear. They eat away at our self-esteem. Standing with our lovers, children, and partners we become rigid in fear that our true nature is one of sinfulness that we are not worthy or our connection to the divine.

The very love and creative energy that would cure all of our feelings of guilt and shame is blocked by our rigid walls of defense, our fears of discovery.

The very concept of desire be it for chocolate ice cream, love, sex, or an intimate relationship with God/Truth, is seen as shameful. One should not desire, but we have been taught to reside in the grey emotional land of never fully experiencing our creative nature and our connection to the divine. Life and consciousness without passion is like a sunrise with the sun always hidden behind grey clouds. Passion adds the excitement,

motivation, and commitment to be connected to all life.

How sad that we put ourselves into these places, hidden from the beauty and bliss of being fully connected. Residing separate, lonely and in pain. When we self-remember we vanquish the guilt and shame and join in the great choir of life singing hosanna to that which is our creator source.

If we are to experience true intimacy we must shed the covering of these stultifying roles, peel the onion and allow our true splendor as consciousness to shine forth. For it is only in this nakedness of being that we will ever be truly known as we so deeply desire... only in this state will our consciousness be penetrated and melded with another. In this state the pain of separateness is gone.

Being naked is the first step in creating a sacred space of existence in all that we do. For in this state we are consciousness aware of itself as consciousness. In this state of nakedness you are whole and perfect. Only the Truth exists, errors, sin, and fear are no longer a part of your expression.

You are in a state of Grace.

Grace unmerited divine assistance given humans for their regeneration or sanctification, a virtue coming from God and a state of sanctification enjoyed through divine grace.   Merriam Webster Dictionary

Sensuality is the language of absolute love.

Sensuality

We think of the body as sensual. We believe that we feel, smell, taste, hear, and see with the body. Actually the body only acts as a conductor to our mind. Our mind then gives instruction to the body and consciousness about the surroundings. Our sensual experience is not located in our body, but in our mind. For instance, the eye does not see the flower. It simply accepts the light being reflected by the flower. This light then sends a message along our neuropath ways to the brain. The mind then recognizes the pattern of light as a flower and sends back accompanying messages.

Our mind, memory, and consciousness give meaning to what we experience through our body. What we believe is what we experience. If we believe that something is hot it will be hot. Firewalkers believe they won't get burned and they don't. Their body responds to their mind telling them it will not be burned.

Our belief about our body is what we are now experiencing. Light, touch, sensation of all sorts travels to our brain where our beliefs and experiences are engaged to give meaning to the sensual input. Your mind holds the experience that gives you sensual pleasure.

Intimacy happens in the mind. If we believe we are separate, guilty, shameful, or ugly we will block our sense of intimacy and only experience small moments of completeness in an intimate way. Intimacy occurs when you know that nothing other than consciousness aware of itself as consciousness exists. All that has gone before, all that appears to be less than you know to be so about the nature of reality is an illusion. Your body is an act of consciousness. Intimacy is an act of consciousness. Creating a sacred space is an act of consciousness. Loving is an act of consciousness. Your world exists as consciousness. The secret to life is as simple as understanding that anything other than love, and sacred caring for others does not exist... All others are the self. Those who appear in our life are our self... consciousness reflecting to us.

Feeling intimate is a sensation, a knowing, a merging of our mind, body, and spirit. When we are in a state of intimacy we feel whole, complete, and aware. This only happens if we can allow our being to be naked and detached from the beliefs that we are purely physical beings. No matter what chemical response we have

with another, it is still a response of the mind. A chemical or hormonal response is the mind giving meaning and understanding of the experience.

Teach yourself to feel with your mind at a conscious level. Feel the curve of the sofa with your mind. Feel the softness of the breeze with your mind. Feel the being of another with your mind. It is through our mind and our consciousness that we feel and become sensual. The senses are the path to nirvana, heaven, and a state of grace. The intellect can show you the path but the senses take you to the state of consciousness that produces intimacy. Feel the sound of music with your mind.

Our sensuality is a great gift. It brings color, sound, and light to our world. If I were to say to the taste of a fresh strawberry is sensuous many would wrinkle there nose or find a distaste in the use of the word. Even in Merriam Webster Dictionary it declares that sensuality is irreligious, indulgent and pertaining to the flesh. This definition presents another dichotomy in consciousness. Seeing, hearing, tasting, feeling are all important aspects of navigating through life. Our senses are mechanisms of perception, *a meaning assigned by Webster's Dictionary.*

As we gain insight into how to think about life, it is important to shift through belief systems that limit and control our ability to embrace the creative aspect of life. The very core of our existence, our life force the divine nature we carry, is kept locked in a box by the myths and concepts of our subconscious mind. The very rigidity of our fear deprives us of being able to embrace our divinity. We refuse to partake of the divine nature that would set us free.

There is no way to be intimate with God/Truth and your divine nature or enter the Kingdom of (heaven), the Promised Land, the Garden of Eden or Nirvana through intellectual endeavor. You can wear hair shirts, beg, and plead... read and think all you want but it will not afford you entrance. Jesus said I say to you in Truth whoever does not receive the kingdom of God like a child will not enter at all.

To become intimate in any circumstance you must be as a child. Children live existentially. They know they are connected to all life and give no thought to separation. For the most part they are not intellectual or abstract until they begin puberty. A child lives sensually enjoying life and feels no guilt or shame about their emotional nakedness. They feel with their mind.

The Truth of us is that we are all children of God/Truth. The very creative process that creates all life is our father/causer and mother/effect. Our reasoning intellect is a process a tool for us to use not an end all. Intelligence is not about IQ or how much we know, but how well we decipher

the conscious patterns that appear in our life.

We must relook at the rules, ethics and morals imposed upon us. The only true laws are the spiritual laws that govern the universe. This is not saying you should do only as you please and that you don't have to pay attention to man made laws. Jesus said Render unto Caesar the things which are Caesar's, and unto God the things that are God's. However, what we think of as ethics and morals are more often than not rules keeping us slaves to the material world, to the land of Pharaoh, Egypt.

This is not a go-a-head to do anything that would hurt another being or destroy that which is not legally yours. To say that sensuality is irreligious and immoral keeps us from being able to explore our intimacy and our divine nature. It keeps us from fully living. It locks us out of the Garden and the Kingdom of God/Truth.

These acts of intimacy are not a singularity, but rather a state of understanding we are... we exist in infinite variety manifesting as a divine choir. The individual steps we take to free ourselves, to become intimate benefits the whole.

The voice of your beloved is not in a physical being but in the consciousness that allows you to hear.

Touch helps create sacred spaces where we heal and grow spiritually

Touch

When I was in China, I was astounded at how free individual and friends were to touch, hold hands, to kiss, and be physically close without overtones of sexuality. In years past, when we seemed to have a more relaxed pace, we had the freedom to touch one another without sexual overtones. Women often brushed each others hair, kissed and touched one another in loving and non sexual ways. Men bonded and still do through a variety of activities. Slapping each other on the back, arm wrestling, and perhaps playing contact sports. All of these activities deal with touch.

We need to be touched to stay healthy; body contact is important for mental, emotional, and physical health. The touch of a loving mother does more to cure a cold or infection than any allopathic prescription. Nurses and doctors have learned that a simple touching of the patient leads them to the path of healing. The emergency rooms of many hospitals use what is called healing touch (nurses and health care professionals who specialize in Reiki healing and other methods called energy work.).Research shows that survival rates shoot up as much as 50% when patients are visited the night before surgery by their surgeons who touch them gently on the arm.

Hospitals use grandmothers to hold and comfort sick babies, whose parents are not available. Touch is an indispensable aspect of healing and well-being. A child who is held and coddled grows strong, happy, and at peace in its world. A child who is held and stroked stays healthy and thrives mentally, emotionally, and physically. When we touch, we can cure many things in our lives and those we love. Perhaps it is this touch that can eventually cure the world of the sickness of heart and soul. Perhaps being touched could cure individuals of the need for power and control.

Touch is a sensual act. Although many of us connect the word sensual with sexual the concept of sensuality happens to us daily in different ways. Seeing, touching, hearing tasting and smelling are all sensual acts, acts of our senses. For most of us, what we touch and smell remains a viable part of our memory. If a memory is connected to a particular smell, we can more easily recall it than if it is just by sight alone. Many times

a therapist will ask a client to try to remember the smells. This helps the client to bring forth a memory they need to recall. The same happens with touch. If you ask a person what a situation felt like, they will recall sensations of touch. Our senses give color, depth, and meaning to what would be a flat grey world.

Touch erases the doubts, the loneliness, and the pain. At the same time gives a deep connection to our world in ways science can't yet explain. We give meaning to what we see, hear, and feel through our skin to our brain. These experiences of touch are registered under many different meanings in our subconscious. These sensations help give meaning to the world we live in by forming our consciousness and beliefs.

Touch: To bring a body part into contact with especially so as to perceive through the tactile sense, handle or feel gently usually with the intent to understand or appreciate;
To lay hands upon with intent to heal, to play on, to perform playing or singing. (Paraphrased from Merriam Webster Dictionary.)

There are, of course, many ways we use the word touch. But in all of these the common thread is a reaching out... effecting through our presence the connection between our-self and others. Touch through the senses, is needed before we can become intimate. The prelude to intimacy

is a kind of foreplay in the form of a dance and a ritual that often includes touching, stroking, smelling, listening, tasting– all acts of sensory touching. Foreplay for friends and students is the same, sharing food, the tastes and smells, reading and evoking memories of loving times. However it is achieved for intimacy to occur there must be sensual interaction of some sort. The mind must be touched in a sensual way. Without touch we can't cross the barriers of fear we have placed in our minds.

We hear with more than our ears. Sound waves hit our skin and we hear; hearing the voice of the lover is important part of arousal to love and sex. Hearing our lover's name, hearing the voice, reading the name or even a phone number can send a cascade of experiences through our brain that brings us to an advanced state of awareness and alertness awaiting the beloved.

Practice sitting and allowing the sounds of music touch your skin... allow your skin to transmit the sound to your brain. Feel the curve of the arm of your favorite chair... feel it with your mind. Let your mind feel the softness of velvet... smell the flowers and fresh smell of grass and trees. Let your mind touch the consciousness of someone in pain. Let your mind touch your child. It is through letting down our barriers to touch that we experience the connections between our consciousness and all life. Our eyes often lie to us; they tell us our body ends and

begins. As mind as consciousness we have no beginning or end. The energy fields that surround us all extend into the universe. Just as the universe is one infinite whole, so are we. We are a part of a never ending field of energy. Touch is happening all the time. We simply close our mind and put up emotional and intellectual barriers. The most thrilling and energizing act is an act of touch. It binds us in a state of acceptance that brings joy, hope, and love.

Intimacy brings Joy. Joy is gladness, happiness, a feeling of gladness unattested. Isn't joy and unattested gladness what we are seeking in love?
The joy of intimacy simply put is the feeling of happiness that occur when we touch, connect and acknowledge the innermost being of another– the "spirit." In this connection we loose the isolation dictated by the beliefs we hold about our body and environment. We may be intimate with our friends, lovers, mates, parents, and children and God/Truth. The more intimate we are with those in our life, the more fulfilled and purposeful our life feels to us.

Touching the Divine

Our over soul reaches to know and experience the divine, which resides in all of us. This need pushes us to greater exploration of our relationships to all existence. The overriding motivation to touch the divine resides within us all. Sometimes it comes out sideways in excessive needs

for power, money, and fame. When you examine these seeming needs you can see that all of these are drives toward a relationship with something greater than what seems to be.

The journey we take is one of self remembering. This is that we remember the Truth of our existence, the core of our being. We are spiritual beings living in a spiritual universe governed by spiritual laws. We cover the core of our being with myths, beliefs, and lack of understanding. We forget that we are the manifestation of Truth/God the divine source of all life.

Like seeing an oasis we believe what we see and are told. We are not taught the truth of our existence thinking our self limited by our birth parents, genetics and education. While our authentic self, our spiritual self, is covered with these layers of false identities it remains true, ready to function in our lives.

Job in the Western bible sees his life as his identity... horrific events destroy his life. This brings him to a point of grief and being distraught where he finally sees the Truth. Once he reconciles his beliefs with the Truth he sees that all life is spiritual that all life emanates from this one source, Truth/God the divine source. And in this he recognizes that all there is, is Truth/God.

He reaches out and touches the divine. In this he discovers that is was always his perception

and lack of remembering his authentic self that caused the problems in his life. When we reach an understanding that all we sense is Truth/God we begin to realize that when we embrace a child, lover, partner or listen to music or touch a flower we are embracing, touching the divinity of life.

Teaching our children that all life is divine, all life a manifestation of Truth/God allows them to know themselves as whole, and complete. It allows us all to know that the only true existence is absolute love no matter what the appearance. Spiritual law teaches us that all life issues forth from a state of fusion... that in this state of fusion we see the action of absolute love.

There is nothing inherently evil or bad about our body or this earth. We are not our body as such but our body allows us to explore and know the creation of Truth/God. In this body in our human state we can transcend our sensory input and know the divine nature of all. It is through the senses we enter into a state of intimacy with the divine. If we deny the body and think of it as evil rather than an instrument of joy we miss the point of humanity.

Holding a new born child and smelling the sweet smell of birth, looking into the eyes of a 4 year old and answering their million questions of what and how... holding the hand of a dying parent... seeing a sunrise... weeping at a sad movie... pas-

sionate loving each moment of our life is being human. Every moment of every day our life is a divine encounter of intimacy. It is what gives us our commitment and helps us form covenant with Truth/God. We are no longer withdrawn or hiding from that which is divine. We embrace that which is reported to us through touching life as all divine.

Breaking the Chains of Isolation

When we create sacred spaces in our life in the search of intimacy we are touching the divine that resides in us all. To become intimate with your concept of the divine, God/Truth you must touch. To be intimate does not mean that you are sexual with another. Sexuality is often sought because individuals do not understand how to be intimate. It is thought that sexual addiction may develop in part because these addicts are not capable of being intimate during any encounter including sexual relations. The most satisfying and spiritual sense of sexuality occurs when intimacy leads to a sexual encounter, and a sacred space is created.

Isolation is to be separate or set about apart from the group or whole to be in an uncombined form, to be free from outside influence, insulated. It is the state of being alone or remote from others. (*Paraphrased from Merriam Webster*) The walls of isolation are only broken by the touch of our mind. Allow your mind to feel the

world around you. In this feeling, the isolation we all encounter will no longer be. When we break the chains of isolation we encounter the genuine family of humanity. We remember our true state of existence. In this we realize that life neither begins or ends with our individuation but that our being adds an incredible joy in the whole.

We seek relationships, intimacy and sexual activity to break away from the feelings of isolation. Some cases of teen pregnancy can be directly linked to wanting to break these emerging feelings of isolation. Feelings of isolation are major contributors to depression and loneliness.

Relationships are the natural association and connection between people and the manner in which people are connected be it marriage, kinship or other influence.

We seek relationships to break the isolation and give our expression in this human form significance and intelligence. There are many spiritual teachers who feel that the concept of relationships are the main lessons we all must learn to awaken to our true state of being. Relationships are relative to the time and understanding of the moment. Relationships and their use of intimacy are different in every society. All relationships require the mind to reach out and touch.

.

We can release ourselves from roles of victim and transgressor into a true state of being, consciousness aware of itself as consciousness, the divine being we are.

Forgiveness

There are many things that can keep us from exploring intimacy in our life such as fear of being known, pain of broken relationships and our inability to let go of past hurts.

Forgiveness of past hurts and transgressions is extremely important in a healthy emotional life and exploring the intimacy of our divine nature. When we feel someone has hurt us, transgressed against us it is often difficult to forgive them. It is even harder to forgive our self for our transgressions against others.

How can we explore being intimate if we are afraid and in pain or holding back our authentic self? Earlier we discussed the necessity of being psychically and emotionally naked to become truly intimate. The lack of forgiveness keeps us shielded from our divine nature, our Truth of being. Freeing ourselves from shame, guilt, and

hurt sets us free to explore and remember our authentic self. It allows us to become intimate with life itself.

Release

Recent investigations into memory tell us that it is possible to change memories. Journals kept over several years reveal that as we add information or experience new things old memories are adjusted and changed to fit our current data bank stored in our subconscious mind.

To us as individuals this means we can give up previous perceptions and beliefs for new understanding and perception. Memories from old hurts and transgressions can be released or modified to fit a new realization of our being as one of a spiritual nature of consciousness.

We can relook at incidents of transgressions and realize that the roles played were based on our awareness at that moment. We can release ourselves from roles of victim and transgressor into a true state of being, consciousness aware of itself as consciousness, the divine being we are. We can realize that there is nothing that can hurt the core of our being. It cannot be taken from us or hurt in any manner. It is omnipotent, ever evenly present without beginning or end, expressing itself eternally in this moment.

In releasing ourselves from these old painful memories we can release others in the same

manner. We realize that they played the necessary roles in our consciousness because we (all) were not free to do anything, but follow our unconscious drives. It is only when we realize that we have the ability to move beyond those memories are we truly free to experience true intimacy. There may be momentary glimpses of intimacy in our life, but only when we release and give up old perceptions are we able to sustain long lasting intimacy with God/Truth.

The reason that forgiveness is often hard is that we continue to hold onto the memory of hurt and pain. It spreads through out subconscious mind tainting relationships and experiences that are not related. In a sense our emotional pains infect our life twisting our vision and perception of absolute love and our relationships with life.

To truly forgive means you must let go of the perception that person, place or idea can hurt the core of your being, Truth. Often our perception of a situation is of that of a young child who sees everything big and controlling. We don't see it or interact in situations with an adult mind and thinking straight. Our inner child raises its head yelling and screaming.

Every situation we can let go of previous perceptions for new understandings of our authentic self. By use of emotions and sensory nature we travel across the desert into the Land of Milk

and Honey. We play out the archetypes of Moses and Joseph in the Western bible. As Moses our intellect understands the spiritual path and how we must act to enter the Kingdom. As Joseph we realize that is has always been a divine state of being. That God/Truth has always been all there is lighting the path to free ourselves form the misunderstanding of the land of materiality.

Forgiving ourselves and others is a sacred act that produces a consciousness that is open and joyfully accepting of absolute love and a state of bliss.

49

Forgiveness

Face your self and your potential. Look at the cosmic, spiritual being you are. This is the beginning of your journey home to a glorious experience of being fully human.

Self

The beginning of all intimacy is the knowledge of self. The exploration of self is learning about your consciousness and the beliefs you carry within. In the world we live in, we often don't take time to know who we really are until there is a breakdown and we are forced to encounter our self. The journey we take is not to learning of ourselves but to uncovering our true self the authentic self as a manifestation of Truth/God. Start with the simple statement of who you are. Do you answer immediately, mother, father, wife, husband, lover, or professional? These are roles we carry and have little to do with our being. They are expressions, to an extent, of our consciousness but are not the totality of our consciousness.

Year after year, you have been growing your consciousness. You may have been planting seeds you are not aware of. The goal of being intimate with yourself is to understand what lies in your

consciousness, to reveal to yourself the fearful secrets you hide from.

To become intimate with yourself, you must stop fearing yourself. We are taught that we are naughty and bad in the Western world. We are taught that there is something inherently wrong and sinful about our being, body, and existence. In some religious circles this is called original sin. Many people feel shame about their bodies and their needs. Hence we make love in the dark and dress out of site of our mates and lovers.

Our bodies and minds, our very world is created out of our consciousness. We know the body is very sensitive to our thinking. This relationship is so sensitive that placebos are 75% effective in research study. It is the belief that helps cure, not the drug or non-drug. Our beliefs about our existence and body are powerful, so powerful they can cause stigmata, miraculous cures, and total freedom from life threatening situations. Your thoughts and beliefs are producing the world you see. Your consciousness is accepting thinking that makes you vulnerable to universal beliefs, which can produce disease and other problems. In this same manner consciousness can free you and heal you from disease. Ask yourself what belief your actions and thoughts are connected to. Ask yourself if this is a belief that is helpful, harmful or simply blocking you

from experiencing the extraordinary being you are.

Pick up a coffee cup with the handle placed to your left. Draw the cup. Turn the cup 90 degrees and draw it again. The useful cup with a handle disappears when you change your view. When you change your view of the world your world changes.

If you are blinded by fear, shame, guilt, and misunderstanding you will not see what is available to you. You will not see those around you who would be intimate with you, bringing comfort, light, and joy into your life. As long as you fear and hide, you cannot be free to know yourself and be intimate in a loving manner with yourself.

The studies on the placebo effect indicate that the mind not only controls your state of health but also learns the behavior of illness. We know that children learn fear and other behaviors from their parents. Your fear, shame, and guilt are learned behaviors. To be fearless we must learn the behavior of the fearless; to be well we must learn the behavior of wellness. We can change our thinking and beliefs so we may act differently with our consciousness. Our consciousness is the Creator. As we free our consciousness from stultifying behavior, habits, and beliefs of limitation, shame, and guilt, a new world opens to us.

A world of joy opens to us. Intimacy starts with the self, with knowing what is in consciousness. With understanding we do what we can do with what we have been taught. You can unlearn the fear, shame, and guilt.

Stand in front of a mirror naked. Don't criticize just look at your body and tell it that it is serving you well. Embrace it. Embrace every part of yourself... tell yourself that you are loved. Observe how you feel. Until you can look at yourself naked, honestly, and openly you can't be intimate with yourself... knowing yourself and allowing yourself to feel love for yourself.

How can we love others, be intimate in a fulfilling manner if we can't experience those feelings for our self? A meaningful relationship isn't possible without intimacy. Intimacy is not possible until you become intimate with yourself, knowing yourself, penetrating your consciousness to the core of your being.

Observe yourself in action. See beyond your ego and beliefs. Face your self and your potential. Look at the cosmic, spiritual being you are. This is the beginning of your journey home to a glorious experience of being fully human. It is in the relationships of your humanity that you will experience God, higher mind, Buddha; – whatever name you have put on the very nature of existence and reality, the name you give your Creator.

Sacred Intimacy

Self

As we become intimate with our authentic self our beloved faces us so we may encounter the Truth of our existence. We find the reflection of our divine core of existence looking back at us from the mirror.

Covenants

The search for love and intimacy carries with it an underlying objective. Unconsciously we know that in love and intimacy we will find the purpose and meaning of our existence. From the moment of our conception to the time of our death we search for meaning and purpose in our daily existence. Instinctively we know that great love carries us beyond our ignorance and misunderstanding of our consciousness.

In our journey to self remembering there a thirst to know what we are about, the why of our existence... the purpose of the life we live. The purpose and meaning in life sustain us in times of our long dark night of self encounter. Our purpose is our beloved. Following us, loving us and knowing us when we would not know ourselves.

As we become intimate with our authentic self our beloved faces us so we may encounter the

Truth of our existence. We find the reflection of our divine core of existence looking back at us from the mirror. This is the most intimate of all relationships. To build this relationship we must be willing to let go of our ego will forces. We must cleanse our consciousness of our guilt, shame, and paranoia if we are to form this merging of for all time.

Covenant: Promises, rituals and commitment to form a pact a merging ... mainly through person and God.

This relationship takes a commitment. This is a covenant between you and the beloved. To be fully committed to this relationship you must have faith and trust in your innate knowing of your spiritual being and the spiritual laws that govern our universe. Stepping beyond conventional beliefs and myths takes a leap of faith and trust.

Standing at the great chasm of life we much each make our personal covenant with the divine beloved we carry. Leaping into the chaotic chasm the greatest miracle of all happens. What was once chaotic and dark becomes harmonious and light... and we have a revelation. The miracle of life, the purpose of being is revealed for the first time the meaning of existence is awakened in our consciousness. In this most extraordinary experience we find our beloved.

Sacred Intimacy

Vulnerable: To be vulnerable is to be susceptible to wounds and gifts.

To experience intimacy to find our beloved self we must become vulnerable to our own spirit and psychic nature. The connecting energy between people is soft and open. If we put up blocks or shields we block out that energy. To be open and vulnerable you must trust your spirit and innate ability to stay safe.

To be vulnerable means you must surrender your ego will to your authentic self. Surrender to Truth/God the divine being you are. In our surrender we find strength. Just as great tees surrender to the wind so must we surrender if we are to be strong and healthy in our life. If we are to honor the spiritual causer of life... we must surrender to the greater will of Truth/God. God/Truth isn't outside of us. We are surrendering to our own being our own divine core.

We become an active conscious member of a great universal chorus of hosanna when we form our covenant and surrendering to our purpose of being... our beloved, our cosmic intent.

Your soul mate is your concept of deity.

God

In the Western world seek a relationship with what we call deity. In the West we have built many churches and formed many communities based on the idea of knowing or being spiritual in nature.

It appears that most relationship-seeking behavior is the search for the spiritual, the reality of life as we see it in another. We never see our own face, we see reflections or what we assume is a reflection in a mirror. We must from by time we are a teenager decide that we exist. The abstract idea of existence comes with both a freedom and a shackle. In establishing our existence we state that we are by simply saying I am. This can be in conjunction with our gender, our roles, and profession. Our use of language reinforces our existence. When we use the form of the word to be we are making statements of our existence. Even to say I don't exist is to say you exist. Before you can't exist you must exist.

We are taught from birth to believe what we see. The old saying "seeing is believing" is a good example of how we are taught that our senses report what is really there. Our existence is always questionable. The exception to this adage is the mirage on the desert caused by a heat inversion. Even small babies will laugh at perspective that is turned around from what we are used to seeing. Look at M.C. Escher's work this will give you insight to how automatic our senses are. Feel with your mind. See differently.

In our teen years we believe that we are separate from our parents and the world. We face the abstract concept of isolation and mortality. In our thinking we feel the urge to see ourselves. The best way seems to be in our reflection of another. In them we see our self, spirit, and Creator. The realization for that moment that we do exist and are not isolated in some hell away from all life comes into our consciousness. We have in that moment realized our God self as we realize and acknowledge the God self of the other.

Because we have been taught to believe our senses we also know that many times they can't be trusted. Thus we seek to know truth and understand what is true in our lives. We seek relationships at an unconscious level so that we may see reflections of our self. We pursue the other so we may find reflections that teach us and give us insight, and understanding into

what and who we are. We seek lovers and companions that lead us to an intimacy with God. At our very first orgasm with another we realize we are whole and perfect and connected to life. The thrill is not just in our senses and body, but in our consciousness we feel our first intimacy with deity.

In Christian philosophy and religion we are taught we are made in the image of God. We see pictures of Jesus and find that he looks human (albeit more English than Middle Eastern). He is the Son of God according to the scriptures in the Bible. He reminds us of our nature. We see God in the other but not in ourselves. We are a species in search of our Creator. We search for a part of our selves we cannot see and fathom from our experience.

We seek the life force that gives us life beyond the body. We have been taught to believe what we see and yet we know that life force is not restricted to objects but animates from another place. We seek to be whole in our understanding and knowing of our being. And in this search we reach out to our fellow beings in search of penetrating and being penetrated so that we may both be understood and know at the same time. At this moment we want to be whole. For without this moment of revelation we feel incomplete, limited, with a beginning and end. We are searching for the infinite and the finite to be

resolved as one. We seek to resolve the paradox of life and our being.

This search to know and be known is the search for our Creator, our purpose and mostly for our God. We are looking for our soul mate. We become confused and think that our soul mate resides in another. We think it is human in form and become embattled and bitter when this appears to be wrong. Moving from one relationship to another we "sin" in our search.

To be whole we must have a relationship with our God, Deity, Higher Mind, our very nature of existence in the image of God. Because we have been taught we are not good, and therefore not God we, cannot accept that we are the Creator of our world that to be intimate with God is to be intimate with our self. To know our self as whole, as the completion without ending of life cannot happen with another until you have had an epiphany of your intimacy with God.

Adam and Eve ran from God in the Garden of Eden. They hid their nakedness and were ashamed. They were ashamed because they became aware that they has disobeyed a law of spirituality:

To know is to know not. No matter what you see with your eyes you are seeing illusion. The knowing of self is the knowing of God. Forever we have been searching for God, Deity, and our

spiritual connection, feeling we have been put out of the Garden of Eden... We search because we think

God is hiding. God your spiritual nature is not hiding. The very life force you see in others is what you seek in yourself. Like Adam and Eve we hide from our spiritual force, Deity and our God self. We cover ourselves in the roles of the ego, in our inhibitions, fears, and guilt. You must uncover yourself and stand naked before the God Creator. Only in this manner can you experience the intimacy with the God self.

Your God self sees beyond all illusion, it sees beyond the lies, the self-deception and seeks that in you, which has always been whole, without sin, that which is truth, that which is true about you. You are a loving being full of insight and understanding. You cannot hide behind clothes, the acting roles you have taken on, the excuses, the victim you often become. You cannot hide because you think you are missing a part of your soul.

That which is so – Truth, God – has always been present. This is the secret of intimacy with God, that which is God, Truth, Higher Mind, Supra Consciousness is always there waiting with open arms for you to embrace the beloved life force. Your true beloved is not another person, but the spiritual being of self. Only in the moment of

God

revelation that you are intimate with your sense of deity at all times will the hunger that haunts your being be fulfilled. Once you know you can't un-know... you can't forget. You can only accept that life force, God has always been in you and always will be.

Like a small child you have turned your face from the Creator self trying to hide. BUT your Creator knows where you are, who you are, and all there is to know. You have only to let down the veils of secrecy, pain, self-torture, and separateness to step from the finite limited life to a limitless life of the joy of intimacy with the deity you seek.

The God center of life waits patiently for time and space do not exist in the nature of reality.

Soul Mates: Spiritual or immortal essence of a relationship. People ideally suited for one another in a variety of relationships. When two people meet and feel as if they have found a "missing piece" of themselves, this is called soul mates. Some metaphysical practitioners believe our soul splits into seven parts at the time of reincarnation. A soul mate may be a lover, mate, or friend.

The only true soul mate is the one you have with yourself and your deity. You have always been in the Garden... Awake! See! Surrender to the loving life available to you.

God

Faith and religion terms are inadequate to describe the reciprocal bond and accessible intimacy and absolute love between humankind and the Creator.

Power

The only true power any of us have is how we choose to love. Taking the responsibility for our true power means we must become responsive to our ability to be intimate and love all of life. Intimacy is true power. In our intimacy we are fully surrendered to the God/Truth. In this surrender we

We live in a world hungry for power and control. Power and control issues are more than issues of any government. They are struggles of individuals in our world. Those who grab for power are not in a place of control or true power but in a place of deficit, of want and need. They need control in order to feel safe, because they cannot trust themselves and their true nature. They have not self-remembered. The need for power and control comes from fear. This is fear of non-survival, fear of loosing some vital part or idea of our self.

Feelings of being weak cannot be overcome with will forces. We cannot survive because we will our survival but must come up higher. To over compensate and dominate does not produce safety or freedom. The only true control any of us have is how we choose to love. Absolute love coupled with intimacy increases your power by a 100%. In a state of sacred intimacy you are truly free. Free to experience absolute love that is endless, timeless expression of our remembered self.

As free individuals we can inter-dimensionally experience and connect to others similar to us. This happens when the chorus, the collective vibration that is sent out through these connections helps to awaken others who are beginning to hear the song we send out. This is the music of the universe... it is us singing hosanna in a great chorus of absolute love and intimacy with all life.

There is NO power, NO we, NO unity and harmony without intimacy and love. The intimacy and absolute love are a great force that is gathering momentum. This beautiful world, universe has begun not its final destination but its true destination. Beauty in the sense of balance and harmony is light that we all carry within us. And in self remembering we free ourselves and those around us to experience this great moment of all time.

Sacred Intimacy

Stand and broadcast your love in a state of intimacy. In intimacy we remain vulnerable to all life God/Truth. In our vulnerable state of surrender we find our strength, and our true self, our beloved is revealed to us.

Spirituality is only known is a state of intimacy, God is only known in a state of intimacy and Truth is only known in a state of intimacy. You cannot be intimate with that you don't know. You can only know from a state of surrender. We surrender our erroneous ideas and beliefs for the Truth… in this we know. This happens in everything from math to God.

When we are intimate there is no oppression, we aren't forced into believing or accepting anything… we know and experience. The rules of the spiritual universe allow us the freedom from oppression and erroneous ideas. We are free to choose love. Beyond our illusion everything is clear and transparent. We know love and choose love… we are beautifully harmonic in our resonance with all life.

The chaotic chasm we have stepped into is no longer chaotic. What we thought we were we aren't we are eternal… fully human and yet not of flesh and blood, but of life force, of absolute love. We come to this chaotic world and quickly forget our origins or true self. We begin to faith rather than experience or know Truth/God.

You can only know and experience through true intimacy. You can't know God, the divine source or Truth on faith. We have faith when we intellectually understand an idea. Experiencing the divine source goes beyond intellect to a much greater state of existence. It is only through a state of intimacy that you can experience absolute love. All other love is a veneer, a counterfeit and unknown that is subject to the whims of the ego will forces. Our seeming acts of love often cover our pain and shame... our guilt because we feel we should be greater than we are.

In self-remembering we learn HOW to love to be intimate with all life. We embrace the beauty of life... We are in a state of unity with the core of our being, our divine nature our God/Truth within. In this state is truly a state of oneness and perfection.

When we learn and experience through our self-remembering we experience the Truth of our being rather than assume an outer identity. When we join we come together with the greatest of passion and desire... we surrender our will forces to that which is whole, complete, and perfect in its expression of absolute love.

Spirituality is expression of absolute love and intimacy. The spiritual laws that rule the universe are the laws of love and intimacy. When we model these to others we stand in a place of

Grace and Truth. We become the embodiment of intimacy and absolute love.

It is impossible to broadcast absolute love and intimacy when we are not free from the old beliefs, myths, and faith we think are our self. For another to share our intimacy and absolute love they too must free themselves from the chaotic beliefs we all carry.

If there is a reason to be born on this planet in this universe it was to experience freedom from the chaotic beliefs we carry at an unconscious level. In freedom of choice you have an infinite number of choices you can make. When we make the choice to love and be intimate it is a profound choice...

Our choice to love all life frees us from forcing our spirituality, our beliefs onto another who has not found the freedom from the ego self. To force our choices on another is a kind of spiritual rape. Until an individual is open and surrendered to the divine core, what we offer often feels aggressive and chaotic. We can only resolve to model our grace, love, and harmonic song so another may find us in their search for self. Until and individual has self remembered they cannot experience absolute love and sacred intimacy.

Faith and religion terms are inadequate to describe the reciprocal bond and accessible intimacy and absolute love between humankind and the Creator. As a collective consciousness our disconnect through not understanding HOW to love and be intimate had us expel our divine feminine nature building foreign gods and creators out of collective and individualistic egos. These foreign gods serve our individual egos, cultural collectives, fetishes for control and power.

These imitation gods project humankind's feelings of incompleteness and wholeness. They (imitation gods) serve the ego's inability to function in a world of absolute love and intimacy.

The Creator source, our divine core, God/Truth has supplied us with the ability to use the spiritual technology of absolute love to bring us into a state of unification as consciousness experiencing the divine nature of all life. We bring forth the light in our acts of absolute love and intimacy.

Power

Spiritual surrender is about learning to let go and accepting life for what it is, not what we wish it could be.

Surrender

Spiritual power is based in an act of surrendering to higher source, to the Creator of all life and what we call Absolute Love.

To surrender is to yield to the power, control, or possession of another upon compulsion or demand; to give (oneself) over to something (as an influence); to give oneself up into the power of another. Surrender is a verb, a movement. It is not static.

Surrender is an important part of understanding intimacy and love. For there to be an experience of purpose and meaning we must surrender (in this case give up) our beliefs about our being. How can we be intimate with another if we think it is all set in the physical state? Intimacy, knowing and being known, happens in the mind, higher mind. You can't hold out against love but must surrender to it and in the

surrendering you find intimacy and sacredness at levels never experienced before.

Spiritual surrender is about learning to let go and accepting life for what it is, not what we wish it could be. We each carry romantic ideas about our deity, lovers, and life. We carry a concept that spiritual reality is perfection. I have learned that the world of perfection is a lie. All life is from the Creator and this life contains the rose as well as the thorn that pricks. If the Creator creates life then all life is from the Creator. We can't have life and non-life in the same moment. All life is creation. Just as our consciousness has created the life we live in so can it create a new life.

When you surrender to the creation of love and intimacy you begin by learning to let go of old beliefs, old pains, old failures for the now existence you are creating. By learning to let go, you aren't quitting or settling for less out of life. Surrendering does not mean that you quit striving and living life. It does mean that you look toward life differently. This type of recognition is a realization of where you are in your life. You begin to understand that you are more than the old beliefs. When you resist letting go of painful situations, anger, and guilt, you hamper yourself from moving forward into relationships that carry new meaning and purpose in your life.

There are several actions we each must take on our way to becoming intimate with our Creator.

Sometimes we take actions in a wholly unconscious manner with an innate knowing this is a direction we must take. Other times we must work up to actions.

Forgiveness, Gratitude, and Surrender are three of these actions. Sages, mystics and holy men have all told of these actions. We must, in this plane of existence, be able to serve two masters, the seeming physical world, dream state, and our divine nature, the reality of that which is so. Serving the physical, dream state, doesn't mean we give into it in such a manner as believing in it. Like the oasis or awakening from a dream we see the Truth and understand it is an illusion. Understanding the physical, dream state, as an illusion frees us from the fear/aggression drives that separate us from our divine core our divine being. In this understanding we are freed in a manner where we self remember our true identity.

In surrendering our illusions to Truth we leap a large chasm of fear. Many of us take small steps afraid of what lays ahead. The unexplored territory of our consciousness can be fearful and hold many unknowns for us. When we surrender the illusions and dream state we are left with one idea... That God/Truth is all there is... and this vastness can be so overwhelming that our ego puts up road blocks.

Surrender

Why the road blocks? The ego is not some awful cruel aspect of our self, but rather our minds inability to comprehend that God is all there is. How can the mind, as we know it, fully accept and comprehend the totality of reality. Our senses and belief system have trained us that there is a finality... to believe in the oasis and the illusion that all there is has beginnings and endings and is finite in nature. We see the turning of the seasons and we believe that this is the passage of time. We can't fully comprehend these things intellectually or emotionally. Our ego, our human nature begs for an endless stream of changeless ideas and concepts. We search for stability thinking this is harmony and balance. We believe and try to comprehend the seeming physical laws of the universe and then rail against the God/Truth when we think we have been tricked.

There is a consistency in spiritual law. It says to let go of the beliefs and understanding that keep you bound to a time filled finite universe. It says to give gratitude or recognize the creator source of our life. It says to forgive our self and others for trespasses against the spiritual essence of life and finally it says to surrender to that which is so, Truth, God and the omnipotence of the totality of reality.

A resistance to surrendering to a higher source makes the journey we take more difficult. Noth-

ing keeps you from letting go other than your own attachment to your ego needs and fears. Ego fights a fierce battle inside of us. The battle within is the battle for the soul. Our soul is always there, whole and perfect. It is our mate, lover, and cosmic intent. For the splendor of our soul to shine forth, we must win the battle the ego wages.

Our ego fears that in surrender, all that seems familiar will be lost. That which is illusion and shadow disappears when the light is turned on. Surrendering to knowing and being known by God is like turning on a million stars. A bright light is cast into the shadowy corners revealing all that has always been and always will be as love and acceptance of being. That which is truth, is true, is all that exists. For that which is NOT truth has no existence in reality. Everything outside of this must be an illusion, an aberration or a dream. For in life that which is so is all that exists. Ego is an illusion created out of fear and pain. In the nature of reality it is but an illusion with no existence other than what we allow it to have. When we surrender misconception, ignorance, hate, anger, and fear are lost to the nothingness from which they came.

As long as we allow the ego to block our path to intimacy and love, to a connection to God, we continue to be a victim of our own pain-filled history and beliefs based on misconceptions

and fear. We become victims of our unconscious destiny forged out of illusion.

As long as we remain a victim of our ego, we live a life devoid of choice. Most of what we think is choice is our ego moving us along a path it feels is safe for maintaining the status quo. You can't be intimate or experience love in a sacred space if you allow the ego to make the choice. The only way around this predicament is to learn to surrender. In surrendering you have made the ultimate choice to disengage from battles that keep you busy and locked in fear. As the Creator of your world, surrender is always an option.

Surrender is sensual, highly erotic, meaning it stimulates the creative urges. Surrendering to intimacy, to God, to Deity is sensual. Your body softens and vulnerability becomes your strength. When you are vulnerable you surrender to the spirit within the deity center of your being. You accept your soul. Instead of pulling back and retracting you allow your mind and energy to flow out at the same time accepting the energy that flows inward. This out to in flow is the secret of the sages, mystics, and priests/priestesses. Only in surrender can you experience true intimacy and absolute love.

All of this requires feelings of safety as you create a sacred space for your intimacy. To be safe is to be free from risk or danger. Safety is a necessary feeling for the expansion of consciousness and the intimacy with God.

Maslow's Hierarchy of Needs places feelings of safety immediately after the need of food, water and shelter. It is impossible to become vulnerable and open to another's love and intimacy if we do not feel safe. Safety in relationships deals with trust and feelings of being cared for in a state of absolute love.

How can you allow another to explore your inner most being if you are afraid? How can you explore your Creator self if you are angry and stiff? To surrender you allow the energy and psychic field around you soften... become pliable. Your focus becomes soft ...

On a personal level you can tell if someone is feeling safe and sensual around you their eyes dilate... their focus softens. Try surrendering in small steps. Try surrendering to a piece of music allowing it to penetrate your very being... hear with your skin, your mind not just your ears. Surrender to the smell of a rose... allowing it to fill your consciousness with the ardor of the flower.

In surrender you stay present. Time does not exist in past or the future. Surrendering is a sacred act. A kind of emotional dance to the music we create when we broadcast as absolute love.

Surrender

Awakening from the dream state we begin to realize that the fulfillment of our earthly desires do not satisfy us. No food fills the gnawing hunger that seeks to know, no sexual encounter satisfies the deepening desire to merge with the creator source and no obsession gives us the power and control we seek.

Passion

In the western world we think of passion and desire connected directly to sexual longing or material concepts. Passion and desire play an important role in our craving for intimacy and absolute love. We carry intense drives that say go beyond our limited view, remember who you are and return to the core of all life. To understand the intimacy and the absolute love we crave we have to understand desire and passion.

Pain is often caused by a resistance to the body, emotions, and spiritual movement of life. To the Buddhists pain is about desiring and not having the desire fulfilled. Desiring and wishing for that which is an illusion causes pain. There is no reality or life in illusion other than the fantasy we attach to it. To desire illusion can be likened to desiring a character in a cartoon to become animated with life entering into your world as a real person. When we resist our spirit (by desiring illusion) or try to separate our self from the nature of reality –Truth, God, Creative Force,

Higher Mind, Deity – we will feel pain. Pain can be spiritual pain or emotional pain; both may result in physical pain.

Attraction and Fantasy

In our teen years we often find we are attracted to the team captain, the beautiful cheerleader or the popular movie star. Our attraction to these types of people has to do with our major sex organ... the mind and the use of fantasy! Men and women fantasize about being loved by those who are powerful and well known. Groupies around famous musical and movie stars are formed out of this fantasy. These musicians and stars often seem to say what we have not learned to verbalize about our own life. They make us feel connected to a greater whole the "ultimate" group. We belong to something greater, more global through our fantasy then just our close circle of associates.

Many of us seem attracted to a certain style of person. Tall, short, dark, fair beautiful, musical the list of attributes we seek in another can be limitless. These attractions are mainly a part of our ability to fantasize about our physical life. Fantasy serves a part in all sexuality; it plays a very small role in the intimate side of a relationship.

There is a great deal of difference between attraction and obsession. In obsession or being obsessive there is a sense of owning and controlling the object of fantasy. Attraction in an actualized relationship deals with "knowing" the psyche of the other.

Desire is intentional. It is the motivational force in all life. Even to wish not to desire we must desire. In true intimacy the state of desire exists and does not exist at the same time. The experience of this is cannot be described in words. It is the place within our consciousness where the birth and death cycle ceases to exist... where we understand the nature or our existence to be eternally present...

Desire plays a major role in our reaching for intimacy. Without the desire and passion we would not reach for a moment of intimacy. For sacred intimacy to be achieved the passionate attachment of the desire must be released. We must reach beyond the desire letting it go for the pinnacle, the climax of sacred dance... where we become Nothing and so all things... where desire no longer resides and yet life is full of desire... where the cycle of birth and death are no longer the most important play in our life.

In desire and fantasy there is nothing bad or good. No judgment is being made about these aspects of our nature. Our goal is understand how to use them to release ourselves from the attachment of the senses. To be attached to the sense says we believe in the illusion. When we are detached we don't give up our sensory perceptions we simply self remember and in doing so become intimate with our divine nature. In detachment we realize the illusion is an illusion and its all a dream... letting the dream fade as we awaken brings us to a truly divine place of being.

Awakening from the dream state we begin to realize that the fulfillment of our earthly desires do not satisfy us. No food fills the gnawing hunger that seeks to know, no sexual encounter satisfies the deepening desire to merge with the creator source and no obsession gives us the power and control we seek.

The more awake we become to the true nature of reality the more intense our desires to self remember and return to the divine core. We grow weary of the cycles of birth and death ... our intensity is passion. It is this intensity of desire, this passion that will take us to the brink of our insanity and allow us to cross over the chasm we so dread. In one final intense passionate moment life ceases and begins at the same moment... we have become intimate with our divine nature.

Epiphanies, revelations, truly spiritual moments are not handed to us in a state without desire... to numb our self to desire and passion is to take away the possibility of intimacy with our divine nature.

Sacred Intimacy

We cannot contemplate how far apart we are,
there is always a way to the place in your heart.
There is always a way in your heart.

Passion

Love is not created out of feelings, emotions, or saying I do. But is the container in which we grow and become intimate with all life.

Absolute Love

Absolute love cannot be known or experienced in ordinary states of consciousness. For most of us, the concept of love is tied with human experiences and emotions. Although absolute love may be accompanied by an emotion such as a sense of joy and bliss it is not a human emotion, nor an emotion label by humanity to fit our concept of God.

We cannot fall out of absolute love, nor can our mothers, fathers, and priests withhold it from us. NO one can give us absolute love and NO one can take it away from us. Now, that we know what it is NOT, what is absolute love?

To find out what absolute love is we need to explore the state of consciousness that allows us to experience it. No words I can write here or class I may teach can give you something you carry within your self. Absolute love is a natural state of being. It is the understanding of the beauty in the Garden of Eden, it is an understanding that God, Truth and spirit don't hide from us but are always present. It is a state of self remembering, where the illusions and dream state vanish into their native nothingness. Once you have a glimmer of this state of being nothing will ever be the same in your life. Just as understanding E=MC2 changed the perception of our world so does the understanding of absolute love.

The experience of absolute love is without intellect or emotion. The state of consciousness and perception leading up to the moment of experience is one of sensual awareness, of great passion. It is only through this state of sensuality, the right usefulness of our senses that we reach nirvana, and the Promised Land. Both are states of consciousness where we experience a continued state of absolute love and the cycles of birth and death cease… we encounter our true nature remembering the self we have always been.

Absolute love can only be experienced in an altered state of awareness. To achieve this state of awareness you must let go of your state of consciousness that deals with good and bad, right and wrong. It is impossible to experience all there is by limiting and dividing your consciousness. As you let go of judging in your life you become more acutely aware of the necessity for the acceptance of all life as consciousness. You are no longer dogged by the haunting memories of isolation and loneliness of not being known. Memories of pain, seemingly inflicted by circumstances and others, pass from you. You may feel very plasmatic, moldable and pliable to

consciousness, vulnerable. It is only in this state of vulnerability, complete openness, that we like the Sophia, can surrender to absolute love.

This state of consciousness is one of feminine energy. It knows no gender in its expression, but as feminine energy it is soft, open and accepting. Just as all women carry the protector energy of the male so do all men carry the vulnerable accepting energy of the female. In our natural state of being we are androgynous. It is this state of androgyny that we enter into the "kingdom of heaven." Our energy our consciousness must reach out as the male with desire and passion know, And our feminine nature must accept the state of absolute love.

This state of absolute love is the "prayer of Christ" the process of alchemy, where we change water to wine, metal to gold. It is the process where we enter into the "kingdom of heaven, or nirvana." It is the one moment in our lives we know, that which is without name and unknowable by the intellect. It is when we become intimate with the divine nature.

To reach this state we must do as Dante did. Enter into the hell of our unconscious mind. Explore the memories and pains knowing that they need not affect our life and release them. As you enter into hell remember the mother self is always with us as is the father protector. When we leave the fires of hell we climb to the mountaintop. Here we receive our true name (nature) and begin to understand that our na-

ture has always been one of absolute love. That is all life all that exist is absolute love no one was ever conceived, no matter what the circumstance, nothing ever created outside of absolute love. It is the creative force of the universe. We come to understand this as our natural state of being, our true state of being. We descend the mountain. In the valley we use our nature for all that will hear and see.

This is the journey we must all take no matter what our path. It is only when we stop hiding from what we really are, when we stop judging our every move, and begin to see that we have always been and will always be for there is no other way to be than as a child of absolute love. We will then hear God Whisper and say I will be with thee forever and ever for today thee has brought forth in love.

Absolute Love

I became acute enough to know that it begins with being intimate with the self. And in this we loose the aloneness, the loneliness and the lack of love we often feel.

Joy

I am not sure what age I lost my innocence, but I am sure what it meant. Not in sexual terms, but rather in loosing a natural concept of existential connections. Until puberty our connections to parents and our environment are effortless and naturally existential. When we leave the age of innocence we must seek our connections. Around 14 years of age abstract thought is triggered by the influx of hormones. The capability of abstract thinking leads most of us to the first encounter with the isolation of our being. We realize we are separate from our mother and other caregivers. We loose the innocence of connection. It is this loss of connection and innocence, which drives us to seek connection, companionship, friendship, lovers and mates. We seek to break free of this isolation in our bodies. We long for emotional love and the touch of another person. We need acceptance and love.

In our mind we find a dichotomy. We long for the expression of our individualism and yet yearn to belong, be apart of a whole relationship be it an individual or a group. In our younger years we may join in sports, clubs and gangs. Within the stereotypical concepts of these we strive for personal-excellence, which fulfills the need for individual recognition and acceptance. Throughout life this pull and tug is a never-ending battle continuing until the concept of intimacy becomes integrated and experienced as part of our spiritual quest. Once we become self-actualized we begin to solve the dichotomy of our being and need for connection.

The Understanding of Intimacy Begins at Birth

We know that a baby does not thrive, grow strong, and happy unless it is held, cuddled, and loved. Even the touch of abuse is better for a child than NO touch at all. And as adults this remains so, we will settle for less than our innate concept of happiness rather than have no touch at all. When I am speaking of touch I do mean physical and emotional/mental touches. As much as we long for a physical touch so do we long to be known by another. We want our spirit to be honored, our mind and emotions to be recognized and accepted.

The greatest gift from a nurturing mother is her ability to express a knowing and understanding of her child as it grows. She gives her child an acceptance of the child's individuation and

spirit of being. A nurturing mother knows her child spiritually, psychically and emotionally. She teaches her children that psychic knowing is the path to absolute love.

Freud misunderstood the wanting to return to the womb. It was not sexual but rather a return by each of us to the innocence of spirit of being totally accepted in a state of absolute love by our mother. In the womb our mothers knew and loved us psychically. Deeply imprinted in our mind and cells is this acceptance of our spirit at a psychic level. Only at the moment of actual birth and our mothers holding us for the first time does is the "physicality of our life" recognized. No baby has a physical realness until this moment of birth.

In our life, the experience in the womb is the foundation for all intimate relationships that are to follow.

The Great Secret of Intimacy

We do not fall in love physically with another... we first fall in love psychically. We touch the spirit of each other, reaching out beyond our chrysalis...to find the JOY of being intimate with the spirit and psyche of another. The moment our spirit touches another, the moment we connect our spirits, the bonds of isolation are

dropped and for however brief we know total acceptance and absolute love. Our being is filled with joy ... we experience bliss and the grace of God and Spirit.

In my life I have had many "intimate" relationships. It is perhaps more honest to say relationships I thought were intimate relationships. In my work I found that we all seek mates and friends that remind us in some manner of our parents (After all what other source of education do we really have in the beginning about intimacy other than our parents?) I sought to be comfortable, safe and loved unconditionally. What I found was not so comfortable nor was it without a horrendous price to my ego and spirit. I found myself being afraid that my looks would diminish and love would not be there. I found myself in abusive relationships. What I did not find was the Joy of Intimacy nor did I find my hunger to be known in an intimate manner fulfilled. Sex was great, but the isolation and barriers only disappeared for short periods of time and then the isolation would return.

I only broke through the fog of aloneness when I became acute enough to know that it begins with being intimate with the self. And in this we loose the aloneness, the loneliness and the lack of love we often feel.
 The secret I have learned is that we only love the spirit of another. We are capable, like good

mothers, of loving all that come across our path. BUT to fall in love to have an intimate relationship means we must be willing to be vulnerable and surrender. In this we will know the other person psychically and allow our self to be known psychically. The rest of the secret is we only fall in love at a spiritual level. All the rest is window dressing.

Love is not created out of feelings, emotions, or saying I do. But is the container in which we grow and become intimate with all life.

The Creator of all life is absolute love.

Relationships

It is hard to pinpoint a starting place with our journey. The complexity of consciousness also holds simplicity of perception. In the uncomplicated way of beginning to embrace intimacy is to begin with relationships. Everything we do is a relationship. We view life and its movement as being something we participate in. This looks like we are separate outside of life. In reality our consciousness is creating the life we see reflecting back to us. We are seeing a reflection of our attitudes and experiences. When we look out there we are also seeing the universal unconsciousness that resides within us.

To know absolute love you must reveal the relationship between your consciousness and your divine core. This is a sacred relationship. To know purpose and meaning you must reveal the relationship between your consciousness and cosmic intent. This too is a sacred relationship. Marriage between two adults is a sacred rela-

tionship, becoming a parent is a sacred relationship. Any relationship with another is sacred and in that sense it is sanctified by God/Truth.

Even the most mundane of tasks reveals a sacred relationship. As it all resonates and comes from the creator source God/Truth. To be truly intimate in our life we must see all of our relationships as sacred and worthy of knowing absolute love.

Healing and bliss don't come from hate, hiding, revenge... they come from absolute love... from the revelation of the authentic being we are. When we surrender to the God/Truth we are healed and find life eternal. That which is spiritual law has no end... just as 2 +2=4 has no beginning or end so is the existence of all spiritual law. Your covenant your contract with reality is this spiritual law, this relationship with the eternal now of all being.

Sacred relationships start by recognizing that all that exists is sacred and blessed as deriving from the divine core of all life. Life takes on a different meaning and is no longer disposable, no longer separate or without meaning. To explore our true self we must see that all life is sacred and worthy of our embrace. To embrace life knowing it is of the creator source and its appearance is simply life manifesting in infinite variety sets us free of the loneliness that haunts our ego mind.

Sacred Intimacy

The sacredness of a relationship is never diminished by separation or the immediate cessation. Love is never ended. We shift and change in our view in consciousness but love remains as does the sacredness of a relationship. The ego may scream, fight, and say it is ended but it never ends. We may grow to dislike the actions of another but the very essence of their being remains in tact.

It is with the essence of being that we love and form sacred relationships. The physical being and actions are a reflection of consciousness of individuals but it is not the core of our being. The essence of us is divine and spirit. We are whole and complete in our essence. Our essence is beautiful and loving. The rest is simply window dressing we have come to believe constitutes the whole of individual. But it is simply a series of roles playing out in consciousness.

What is real is invisible to the eye, but seen by the heart.

It seems that all of humanity hopes that a relationship will make them happy. It comes with the big IF. IF I can only get it right, find the right person, find the right circumstances I will be happy and settled.
We do meet the right person(s) and find the right circumstance(s) and we get it right all the time.

We meet someone and we know it is right... love them totally, completely for a few minutes anyway. Our expectations often outlive the actual relationship.

Must of us are brought up to think that being in a relationship gave you a solid foundation and support system where you grew together. And perhaps there are a few individuals this works for... but for most of us we needed to understand something different.

All relationships are built on shifting sands. We grow and change daily. We come together with our current consciousness, awareness of what life holds for us at this point. Consciousness is like shifting sand in that it unfolds and changes with the slightest input. It adds to our unconscious data base and shifts the very core of our experience and how we experience our world.

I kept thinking there had to be some sort of axiomatic foundation that was changeless in a relationship... and of course there is, just not what most of us had been taught. Couples of all combinations with a long time history have some commonalities that MAY explain their continued relationship.

First the chemical attraction in all relationships ends or shifts after a few months. We either become accustomed to the feelings or our systems

change. So chemistry shifts through the years. The sex between partners can remain good, but not as exciting. The chemistry is replaced by intimacy. Intimacy is not particularly sexual in nature. We can be intimate with many people and find satisfying relationships that are not romantic or sexual in nature.

The intimacy between romantic partners special, sacred spaces are created when the individuals enter unafraid of judgment and rejection no matter what the circumstances. Intimacy at this level is such that we become bonded with the spirit the divine core of our partner. We are filled with compassion for one another. Compassion is where we can hold both our pain and love at the same time. The paradox of loving another no matter what kind of asshole they are being or what kind of pain they are causing.

Compassion and intimacy are only two of the axiomatic ideas present in relationships. After awhile the idea of "I love you" takes on a new meaning or a different meaning. The binding and intimacy take the couple to a new level where it is hard to recognize love in an ordinary way. Something else has happened. In the shifting of consciousness in the relationship a true secret is revealed.

Couples who are willing to embrace the divine core of each other find they live differently. Their

relationship does not produce love, but rather they find that they are living in a vessel of love, absolute love.

Out of their life in this vessel of absolute love comes a wonderful experience they find they are no longer isolated in their consciousness. The separateness we all long to go beyond is no more. In many ways our existence is not two coming together but rather one ... one not producing love but one experiencing absolute love, the foundation of the universe.

A perfect relationship is a lie. There are no rose gardens of perfection. Every relationship has ups and downs, arguments of silly things... pain and pleasure. Our fantasy and projection of what we think our partner should be causes most of the problems in our relationships. Those who can stand naked and unafraid before lovers, exploring a sacred space of intimacy access this vessel.

The principle of absolute love is of course genderless. It is ever evenly present through out the universe, whole and complete and perfect in a divine sense. Experience it for a moment, a month or a life time... but take time to explore the vessel of absolute love that is accessible for us all.

Let go of the perfect syndrome and start living the reality you are... absolute love.

Sacred Intimacy

Like most important concepts of humanity, such as our psychic ability, mothering and absolute love, relationships often get the short end of the talking stick. We seem to speak in terms of others and attributes we want in our life, but rarely ever do we speak about the dynamics necessary for a relationship that is fulfilling and worthy of the effort it takes to maintain an intimacy.

These principles are not meant as have to do rules but rather guiding concepts. Over the years I have observed many habits, approaches and states of awareness in my self and those who came to me for council. I have found these principles to be somewhat axiomatic in that they seem to sustain themselves in a variety of situations and relationships.

Spiritual law, axiomatic Truths don't say that relationships of any sort are to make you happy. Happiness is a dynamic of self-remembering. Happiness is a state of consciousness where in we accept and are intimate with all life. Relationships of all sort present pathways to reach these states of consciousness.

No one, no one, other than yourself, can make you happy. We are responsible for our own consciousness, our own emotions. As we self remember our consciousness becomes actualized and in this we have choice. We can choose peace, joy, and bliss. This doesn't mean we deny pain

and suffering but we look at pain and suffering to see where we are attached to false identities.

Attachment to the ego identities causes pain and suffering. As Holy Spirit seeks to disengage us from these illusions, the ego, we, feel the pain and we suffer. When we know our true identity we no longer suffer.

All pain and suffering can be looked at as an attachment to an illusion a desire to remain earthbound rather than stepping into our divine nature and accept that we are children of the Creator of all life. The essence of us isn't illusion but Truth.

When we surrender the ego, pain and suffering to Truth we become free. Free to choose happiness. Only in acts of sacred surrender can we obtain true intimacy with life.

Friendship: A helper or sympathizer a person with whom we hold mutual respect and affection. Friends come in many different levels we can have deep friends, casual friends and friends that fulfill soul needs. The development of friendships gives our lives meaning and connections. Friends often reflect our consciousness back to us helping us to grow spiritually.

Sexuality: Creative energy. Formless, timeless and dimensionless force, expressing in an infinite variety. Having to do with creation and procreation.

Sacred Intimacy

Creative impulses are present in every relationship. Our use of sexuality is dictated in its use by our past experiences, society's concepts and how our parents taught us. Coition is neither more or less an expression of sexuality than playing a piano, writing a book, painting a picture, cooking a meal, or any other creative endeavor. We use our sexual energy every day in a variety of ways.

We place our hopes and dreams of the perfect mate or friend. The best-kept secret of all is that there are no perfect relationships, no perfect mates, and no perfect friends.

Relationships, true love and compassion reside on the chasm of insanity. The shifting sands of consciousness change a relationship daily. Shifting consciousness changes the direction and atmosphere of our relationships. Even if we are in tune we think we are there are going to be periods of discomfort. There are times when our dreams and fantasies are dashed. And we loose hope.

Relationships are about the spaces between us as well as the spaces we share... The space between defines the vibration and how we unfold. A sound or vibration is formed as much by the stops and empty places as the filled notes.

When we read black type on a white page we

are not reading the black, but rather the spaces between and the relationship they hold in our mind. These spaces and relationships form the meaning of the sentences.

Any relationship is formed as much by the spaces we create between us and the object of the relationship as it is by the individual's spirit. Our relationship with God/Truth also contains meaningful spaces in our consciousness. When we allow these spaces to become sacred we build an intimate rapport.

The romance and excitement of any new connection fades after awhile. This includes the discovery of self remembering our true identity... There is a romantic aspect to all relationships. What doesn't fade is intimacy. If you look at long time friends and mates the one constant is their ability to be intimate with each other. They have formed a relationship on intimacy that far out lived the romantic encounter.

There is a romance between God, Truth and our self. We dance the dance trying to entice the divine nature to us, sing our songs and pray our prayers. Rapture is often the accumulation of this romantic dance.

As with all other relationship our relationship with the divine, God/Truth shifts like the grains of sand as our consciousness grows and unfolds to a greater realization that all there is, is Truth/God.

Sacred Intimacy

Perfection is often a human illusion. Divine perfection simply means that all life is God/Truth no matter how it appears. And in this it is whole, complete and perfect. There is no human perfection as it is always based on illusion. No perfect smile, no perfect laugh or body. That is an illusion. Perfection resides only within the sacred space of our relationship with Truth/God.

Relationships may last for a minute or a lifetime. There aren't right or wrong length of times for active relationships.

The paradigm for our relationships starts before birth and continues through out our youth. We look to our parents as role models. Look to the subtle aspects of your parents and their relationships to better understand your own.

The spirit of another is whole complete and perfect. When we fall in love we love the potential and spirit of the other. In actual day-to-day life we encounter the not so perfect aspect of the unconscious mind of our friends, mates and lovers. The unconscious mind may keep the spirit hidden and block our real nature in our connections. The need to control in a relationship is exacerbated by our lack of security and feelings of safety.

Relationships change according to the consciousness change of individuals. The energy of individuals changes in a relationship. The relationship is a dynamic expression much different than just the sum of the parts (individuals). As you try to understand the energetic aspect of a mate or friend so must you try to understand the same aspect of the relationship. The best pairings in relationships are those based on psychic pairing and understanding.

To be intimately connected is to be open and vulnerable to your own spirit. When we stop looking and start accepting ourselves as spirit we find those who are to be our mates and lovers. Once you are connected to an individual you are connected for an eternity. We can simply set aside a direct line or feeling of the other or filter out the intensity.

During sexual relations we accept all there is about our partner including the unconscious mind and its programming. A relationship can add to your expression but does not fill any void in your life. Only your understanding of your self can fulfill the voids.

No one person or idea is so isolated that it is the "whole" world. We need many relationships and friendships to fulfill our longing for connections.
As in all life, we are susceptible to the energy we give out. All energy sent returns to the sender. Treat all you know with compassion and respect and it will be returned to you.

Sacred Intimacy

A relationship with your divine nature is not much different than the relationship you have with your partner, love, mate or children. It starts with loving your self, with finding your internal sacred space and becoming intimate with your self. That is remembering the true self, the essence of all life as absolute love.

The spaces, sacred spaces are simply the vessel for sacred intimacy, the realization that all life is eternal and perfect as it appears. We forge our consciousness out of our beliefs and understandings of absolute love.

Our desires and passions are spiritual in nature. Sexual desire is as much spiritual as is the desire to be one with our divine core. That which is eternal is without beginning or end. We don't reach a plateau and know all there is to know. We don't find the perfect relationship and stop striving to self remember.

No commitment, gesture or words can bring you to the fulfillment of the passionate fires that burn within. When we allow absolute love to become the vessel we live in... we fulfill the longing of spirit to be known in a sacred space. We become intimate with our Creator.
To know for one second that all life is a sacred relationship is to experience God/ Truth. We are conceived in love, born of love and end the cycle of birth and death in love.

The Creator of all life is absolute love.

Relatioships

In Conclusion

It has given me great joy to write this book. It was started almost 10 years ago. I had to learn many lessons before the words could be shared. It appears to me that if we could allow ourselves to be loved, and love, be intimate and dwell in a sacred place with those we love... all of our worries and troubles would vanish. That of course is polyanna, but maybe not... maybe just loving can cure us of the voids and the long sojourns in the hot desert. Maybe loving and being loved can take away the insanity...

It is my hope that sharing these words with you... will awaken a long forgotten knowing of love and intimacy... and if it is awaken already... perhaps these words have added something of meaning. Whatever your journey may it be filled with absolute love and JOY ... may there be moments of sacred intimacy...

Namaste

You may write me at suzannedeak@gmail.com

Silk and Sandlewood...

Hand reaching out gently touching, touching.. looking and feeling.. hand never finding just touching.. silk to the touch.. cool.. reaching and touching.. looking for you.. for some one.. to know.. reaching and touching.. finding heart...

Silently the tears fall upon the reaching hand... finding heart...tears of JOY at the discovery of Heart... tears of love and tears of relief in being known by you. Silent reaching out gently touching, touching this being I thought did not exist.

Reaching, reaching to touch ... the timeless being of my soul... feet upon the path of all time... Heart upon the star that is forever.

Fall 2002

For Tim

Colophon

set in

Georgia
AprendizCaligrafico

Using Adobe Indesign
Printed USA

www.onespiritpress.com
onespiritpress@gmail.com

www.ingramcontent.com/pod-product-compliance
Lightning Source LLC
LaVergne TN
LVHW011424080426
835512LV00005B/248